Chus Pato
~~At~~ the Limit

Chus Pato

~~At~~ the Limit
Inaugural Speech Upon Her Investiture into the Royal Galician Academy

September 23, 2017

Auditorium, IES Otero Pedrayo
Ourense, Galicia

translated by Erín Moure

Zat-So Productions

flies in the face of reason

"Baixo o límite" Original Galician © María Xesús Pato (Chus Pato) Díaz and the Real Academia Galega, Galicia, Spain

English translation © Erín Moure 2018

Translated and published in Montreal with permission of Chus Pato and the RAG.
Photos used by permission.

ISBN: 978-0-9867595-3-6
Small updates and corrections 23 June 2019.
A limited time edition.

Zat-So Productions

flies in the face of reason

Director: Elisa Sampedrín
zatso.productions@gmail.com

Your Excellency, President of the Royal Galician Academy,
Distinguished members of the Academy,
Dear friends who have come to listen:

My inaugural speech today to this Academy will try to explore several questions that have been on my mind with respect to the poem and to poetry, without offering conclusions or theories.

What I have to say has two wings united by a body, so has the form of an insect I love: the butterfly.

One wing will focus on voice, on the relation between biography and writing, the impossible concordance between the sonic and the conceptual, and on the poem as affirmation, testimony, residue that resists, or ruin.

The second wing gathers thoughts on the figure and on limits, on time, truth, great art or the great poem, on the sublime, on the eidetic apprehension of the poem—conceived Platonically, and on how to forge an exit to all this seeking.

The Voice

Let's imagine the following scenario: in it we walk down a street of wide perspectives, so that in the distance, where our street gives onto a plaza, we can see the light of the sky, light that even now is so full of water that it seems a curtain, a fabric with the consistency of ash and the silver of an Atlantic dawn.

Let's imagine this curtain so as to embody something invisible, the voice. Our voice is unseen, and if we wish to speak of the voice and set it before our eyes we have to do it with an image, embodying the invisible in something that we can see and so we say: "the voice is like a curtain of light and water." We could choose another representation, of course, but what is important right now is that we are able to imagine, to set forth the invisible, time, air... in this case the voice. I want to speak to you of the voice, of the voice, firstly, not of speech: of the voice liberated of speech, the voice that announces a possibility prior to all saying and even all possibility of saying, the voice that touches us, that caresses us or bellows at us wordlessly, quietly, in the silence of the cry, of exclamation or admiration, a voice ignorant of articulating words and of writing. Emotive sonic material, the voice, always fugitive, condemned to oblivion, utterly unable to leave marks that would give it something like a future, the voice that is pure insignificant sound, this voice, always erased, vanished, thus indentured and impersonal, vibration produced in the vocal cords by the air of breathing.

Who speaks with that voice? To whose name can we assign it?

Let's imagine again, this time, thousands of needles that from north to south, east to west, in every direction, gather, stitch, and weave this curtain which is the voice, articulating words in that voice, so that someone, anyone can ask:

How far is the fir tree from the cloud?
Or
How many steps am I from the fir?

Millennia pass over the voice, over the words and once again the needles return to poke into and embroider the fabric of the voice, the oral fabric articulated in the voice, then someone, anyone, writes

Cloud

Fir

A well-known paragraph in Aristotle's *Politics* explains that ours is the only animal species that does not have voice.[1] We have speech, and this is precisely what distinguishes us, for in abandoning voice we efface the animal; we abandon the voice so as to learn what is useful and what is not, what is just and what is not, and we define ourselves as speakers. We are those who live and are gifted with language and this speech is our ethics; thus someone, anyone can ask: what does it mean for a living creature to lack voice and yet to speak? And what does it mean for a living being to write?

For Heraclitus, the voice is an invisible harmony that to him is more powerful than the visible; it is an articulation that fades and is preserved at the same time. We thus are living beings who both efface and conserve the voice as something unspoken in articulated language.

---

[1] Aristotle. *Politics,* Transl. H. Rackham. Cambridge, MA: Harvard U Press, 1944. 1.1253a.

The grammarians of antiquity excluded the voice from grammar. They called the voice of animals confused and used the term *engrámatos* (εγγράματος) for that voice which could be transcribed. The first was illiterate and the second was, clearly, a literate voice.

Vanishing in the literate, this voice of the animal is transformed into speech, into articulated language, and only when it is extinguished in articulation is it possible to return to the confused site where the voice is born. We could say that it feels as if biology is transmuted, or transfigured, in speech.

The excision of language into two planes that cannot be reduced to each other is present in all Western thinking, from the Aristotelian opposition described above to the duality of *Sage* and

Sprache in Heidegger,[2] and to Wittgenstein's duality of *showing* and *saying*.[3]

Modern linguistics takes on this duality as an opposition between *language* and *speaking* (*langue* and *parole*, in Saussure and in Benveniste), with the phoneme as the bridge between them that opens and makes signification and discourse possible; Jakobson rightly points here to ontology.

Jean-Luc Nancy (*À l'écoute*) wondered if the voice, and the sonorous in general, is something with which philosophy is fit to contend or if *listening* had been

---

[2] Martin Heidegger. *On the Way to Language*. Transl. Peter Hertz. NY: Harper & Row, 1982.

[3] Ludwig Wittgenstein. *Tractatus Logico-philosophicus*. Transl. Pears/McGuinness. London: Kegan Paul, 1922. (For a side-by-side-by-side edition with original German and both Ogden/Ramsey and Pears/McGuinness translations: http://writing.upenn.edu/library/Wittgenstein-Tractatus.pdf)

replaced by *understanding*. He asks if the philosopher might be someone who understands everything but cannot listen, and does so to be able to philosophize. On one hand, there is the gaze: figure, idea, presence, and on the other the sonorous that lacks form, appears and fades into its permanence, arrives and is not there.

Listening exists in relation to understanding; as such, in all understanding the voice, that nonform, exists, and in every truth the sonorous lives, the unformed, the transitory, the coming and going of the voice.

To sound is to vibrate. We might say that light is instantaneous and that sound is propagated. The voice is of the order of participation, of contagion; it gives us a capacity unlike any other. It is an incalculable affect: it is extended, penetrates, arrives and is dilated or deferred, or it is transferred, the voice is the wave of tides. It puts a column of air into vibration, a column of flesh; in it we listen to ourselves: in the howl, in song, in the word exclaiming just as did our first cry at birth.

In the voice we hear that which, unsaid, is other than the said. Perhaps we never hear anything but that which cannot be codified and we understand nothing but that which, already codified, we can decodify. We hear love, desire, passion, happiness, grief, courage. Perhaps we hear only the incommunicable which is no different from communication itself, that thing by means of which the subject arrives and absents itself in its own coming and going and leaving, so that Nancy writes: "...this skin stretched over its own sonorous cavity, this belly that listens to itself and strays away into itself while listening to the world and while straying in all directions... my body beaten by its sense of body, what we used to call its soul."[4]

Let's ask with the philosopher — and the question is already vertiginous — does the voice resonate?

In the voice, in its *sacrifice*, in its annulation, lies the very possibility of articulated language and, in consequence, of the dichotomies of nature and culture, of what can be said and what not. Perhaps we might think of a humanity that in returning to itself abandons this figure to present itself as touched by the animal *sapiens* and its distinctions, in a dimension in which nature and culture intermix. In this way we might assume the weight of bare life, and not abandon the animal to an inherent violence and unsayability.

---

[4] *Listening*. Jean-Luc Nancy, transl. by Charlotte Mandell. NYC: Fordham U Press, 2007, 43.

As Giorgio Agamben says *(Il linguaggio e la morte)*: "ethos, humanity's own, is not something unspeakable or *sacer,* that must remain unsaid in all praxis and human speech. Neither is it nothingness, whose nullity serves as a basis for the arbitrariness and violence of social action. Rather, it is social praxis itself, and human speech itself, which have become transparent to themselves."[5]

---

[5] *Language and Death: The Place of Negativity.* Giorgio Agamben. transl. Karen E. Pinkus. Minneapolis: U Minnesota Press, 2006, 106.

Writing and Biography: The Language of the Poem

So, then, is articulated language, speech, or writing an art or technique of the species *sapiens*, or are we the fruit of language? In other words, what matters in a poem: life (biography, experience) or language?

From the theological standpoint, the primacy of the logos indicates that the privilege of the signifier, of language, the letter, and origin is revealed to us as trace, as imprint.

In the Gospel of Saint John we read that life is in the word and abides there, inseparable and intimate.

Ancient rhetoric tells us that *ratio* or *ars inveniendi, inventio,* is an access to the site (topos) of the words that are best suited to the argument (topic) in question and will furnish us reasons. This would involve a mnemonics, a conjunction of images that secure us in acting as poets or orators.

Saint Augustine (*De Trinitate*) interpreted *inventio* as *in id venire quod quaeritur* (to cause what is most desired to come to be); as such, what we seek to find in the word is a loving desire for knowledge, in which language is to us a fabric that weaves, in equal parts, love, word, and knowledge.

This Augustinian argument was reinterpreted by the Provençal poets, and we'll now pause to examine this new interpretation, as it gave rise to modern European poetry.

The first troubadours had no desire to learn a catalogue of *topics* or arguments; they wanted to experience the celebration of language as *topos*, as a site they conceived as an interweaving of love, word, and knowledge; they called it their *Dictamen*.

Razzo or *Dictamen* is neither biographical event nor linguistic experience; it is an undifferentiated zone of the lived and the poeticized, an experience of the word as inexhaustible amorous experience.

Love is the name of this experience and, as such, love is their *razzo de trobar* — impulse for poeticizing —par excellence.

To write or sing, to poeticize — *trobar* — is to locate, surround, spin round, return upon something, circle behind, encircle the word, return to it.

Some might now ask: is it the poem that invents Beatrice or is the Lady the one who wrote the poem?

Some will respond that a successful poem is one that melds with life, leaving no residue, and some will opine that it is in the absence of relation with lived experience that the poem's excellence lies. For the first ones, poetry must serve and be subject to the necessities that mark life in a given epoch, must be didactic, this, yes. The second ones conceive poetry as aesthetic artefact, as a construction in which language convokes, through various processes, a melodic lineation and a conceptual conjunction, the exactitude of a metaphor, for example. We cannot escape, however, the fact that this second option is not free of reference to the biographic vector that it negates.

To these two ways of enacting we can add a third which holds that, although poetry and life infinitely diverge on the planes of biography and psychology, they meet again at the point of their reciprocal de-objectivization, re-encountering each other through the mediation of the language that is proper to poetry.

What language is this that is proper to poetry? How is it similar to or different from other uses of language?

As you well know, language has its common uses: those that describe the world (this is a butterfly), those that are an expression of the I (I love the butterfly), and the conjunction of propositions which think the world (there is a butterfly).

The *Dictamen* of love provides an experience of fusion between the lived and the poeticized, and it is recorded in words; while still being the same as the other two uses of the language, and traversing these uses, it differs from them as it establishes the words of the poem.

I'll call this particular language — which is and is not one with the two most common uses — the language of the poem, a language that in reality is a poverty, one that, though poor in words, knows they are life and promises to seek them, bear them onward. Naturally, at the same time, it decides which particular language's or languages' path or paths it must follow in its search. Of all the characteristics that define this language of the poem, I'll highlight two:

- Intensity, an intensity that allows the poem, a thing limited by a form, to open itself to the a-formal, which is to say the absolute, to that which lacks form and limits, in other words, an intensity that allows a measurable thing to touch, contact or caress what cannot be measured:

    an intensity that allows it to write, read, and speak itself at the furthest limit of our capacity as speakers.

- Its capacity to border on the limits of other writing, whether dramaturgy, narrative, science, filmscript, logical, melodic or numeric structures, and also those of other arts, whether sculptural, pictorial, etc.

In reality, this language in which a poem is written is, I think, the matrix of all others that compose any particular language, so that its words emerge exactly when we are without words; we all know this sensation of not having words, lacking words, being mute, and of remaining without words. The poem commences here, in the muteness that erases all articulated capacity of the voice. In such moments, we have the voice at our disposal, the voice that is effaced and articulated, and we can exclaim, admire, or cry out in panic or pleasure; there when we've lost our footing is where writing begins, that language which is of the poem. It's easy to understand, given this, that the words that are poetry's remain outside judgement, can't be interpreted, can't be examined by criticism or theory; "outside judgement" in this context means they are under the spell that caused the abbot Ero of Armenteira to not realize the passage of three hundred years as he listened, simply listened, to the song of one little bird. Regardless of what they write, is it that these words — be they of love or misfortune, or of the worst calamities we can suffer: storm, war, death — always emerge unscathed, and not exactly because they are paradisiacal or configured like Adam's first language in paradise, but even earlier than this: they are Babelian and unscathed, forgotten in themselves, unscathed in their own oblivion, immemorial? All this may be.

The existence of this language of the poem is what continually creates confusion around poetry, which is not produced as are other scientific or humanist texts. We forget that languages are spoken in very diverse ways, each with its own rules; to speak/write one of these languages is to know those rules, which is how the comparison with a game arises: in a given language game, if the rules aren't followed, you're out. In general, and particularly with regard to poetry, all of this is ignored and people believe instead that, given that we all know how to speak and write, poetry should be easy and quick to understand, and then readers feel rejected by the poem, find themselves more often than not with a text that is indecipherable to them. No one advised them that the poem is a language that is millennia old, a language that lives inside languages and that has the honour of writing them without repeating itself in the sort of eternal return described by Deleuze

(Repetition and Difference). No one bothered to tell them that the poem very much precedes the modern institution we call Literature or literary field, and that it has been conducting its life outside it for millennia.

It would be pushing things for me to adopt the idea that poetry is the objective of the species, but I know for certain that what we call the voice of the Muse is, in reality, the speaking of the language. Language is not an instrument of the poem; the poem is one means that a language uses to survive. Each individual language lives through its poets, and the poem repeatedly lifts the writing of a poet further than what he or she was able to suspect; this is the interval in which the future of the language invades the present.

This said, I wanted to defend here the right of the young to learn this future of the language, to be educated in the art of poetry, and defend the right to study how to write poetry at university if people so desire. For this, we need professors to teach poetry and, as in other universities on the planet, to disseminate the work of poets already "renowned" so that the young can lay claim to their inheritance.

I'll stop short of saying to you that the poet is one who creates a life in words. This life, this living thing that is the poem, detaches itself from the lived experience of the author just as it does from conventional uses of language.

Metaphor: An Impossible Concordance

We'll now examine the poem more closely not from a convergence, but from an excision, a disconnection: first we'll recall a place, a common topos, which explains to us that language can speak what it does not understood and the intellect can comprehend what it knows not how to speak. Neurology and the cognitive sciences today generally agree upon the existence of two modes of thought, and on the fact that one of them is not dependent on language.

I hold that, in poetic enunciation, the following takes place: the movement of language, music, discipline, and measure toward meaning is traversed by a counter-song that moves from the conceptual chain, from signification, from the invention of logic, toward the word, without either movement completing the entire trajectory or nestling in each other, but conducting something like an asymptote in both directions. This chiasmus is what I will call poetry, and in it, as at every intersection, a catastrophe can happen, as that little hedgehog (fragment: Jena Circle, Derrida) tries to cross a freeway of five lanes in each direction: the freeways of music and philosophical invention are perilous, yes, for the poem.

I hold that a poem would be that place in language in which melody and concept reveal the impossibility of their coinciding.

The poem would be that place where the intelligence goes dark in names and names play at hiding in intelligence. It is a reciprocal catastrophe of the extremes or edges of language, of its melodic being and its thinking being.

The poem is a living thing that is established in or, better, is based upon the conjunction of an impossibility, an object whose perfection is only possible thanks to its imperfection.

> A *bolt of dark lightning*,
> as Pondal put it
> The *black milk of daybreak*,
> as Celan transmitted

Here I remind you of Paul Valéry's well-known definition: "a poem — this prolonged hesitation between sound and sense."[6]

It takes place because the only thing that can get past the shoals or furthest limits of a language is its own desire to be music free of all signification, or be a pure thought

---

[6] Paul Valéry, *Rhumbs*, in *Tel Quel, Œuvres, Vol II*. Paris: Pléiade, 1960, 636-7. "Le poème — cette *hésitation prolongée* entre le son et le sens."

of its own thinking, a cipher, a mathematics.

In reading many of the texts of poetry of the 20th and 21st centuries, it might be thought that their writing is based on a method similar to the collages of the cubist avant-garde or of dada and it would be legitimate to accede to such a temptation, but all in all, to me, this is not the horizon that might explain the construction of the poem. The ideal for all poetry, to my mind, would be, rather, that which Benjamin called the dialectical image, a notion that arose at the time of the historic avant-gardes.

As you know, a dialectical image starts with two notions that confront each other, two contraries; the image does not form because term A sheds light on term B, or because term B does the same to term A, it happens when in a fulminous way A and B are united and detained in a self-determined monad, in a constellation.

Unlike in a Hegelian dialectic, no synthesis is produced here, no absorption of the opposites in a new proposition that sets the dialectical path in motion again. That there was no synthesis was what bothered Adorno so much; for his part, Benjamin was interested in the halt and not in the movement, in the detention, in which the terms are not absorbed by each other. Benjamin opted for the tension, the polarization of the parts.

Far from conceiving this halt or syncope as quietude, he saw it as a tremour, as the caesura necessary for the impossibility of the possible to come into existence, because this kind of thinking is not argumentative, but given by analogy, by mimesis, by metaphor.

We can compare this image — to clarify this detention — with the stability of scales: the needle is still, but its stability is a tremour; or (in the simile proposed by Aristotle) to the panicked flight of an army that returns to combat formation when one soldier stops: his abrupt halt makes all of them turn back to the field of battle. Or, if we wish, there is the pendular oscillation of the trapeze artist high above who, in the spotlight and immobile on her trapeze, never ceases to move.

It is as horizon and ideal that I translate the proposition of Benjamin to the poem. The poem provides a union of opposites, of counterposed materials not meant to be joined in synthesis, but which, in their detention, their caesura, allow a contemporaneity of language to be written that moves thinking into a space beyond argumentation, via the incalculable entity that is metaphor. Metaphor does not demonstrate the similarity of contraries but their irreducible difference: the lips will never be coral, but for a fleeting moment it seems that what is dislocated can unite.

As such, the poem does not advance from argument to argument, but exposes itself from threshold to threshold, from sill to sill.

Poem as Residue or Ruin

The philosopher Giorgio Agamben employs a syllogism to express his idea of what the human is. It's a phrase of the type — and I cite from memory — "The human is that being whose humanity has been integrally destroyed" (he refers here to humanity in Auschwitz,[7] humanity reduced to fat for soap, superphos-phate for floors, wallets and shoes for sale...). I borrowed this method to move forward, substituting "poet" for "human" (in the sense that all poetry has been destroyed and keeps on being destroyed in Auschwitz, Hiroshima, the Spanish Civil War of 1936-39,

---

[7] Giorgio Agamben. *Remnants of Auschwitz: The Witness and the Archive*, transl. from Italian by Daniel Heller-Rozen. NY: Zone Books, 1999, 58. Pato paraphrases in remembering; Agamben refers to the figure of the *musulman* in Auschwitz to indicate, in short, that the human is that one whose humanity is almost utterly destroyed.

every day, every minute and second of our lives... while the idea of battle hovers over all battles, indifferent to the suffering of those caught in battle). From this there emerges a definition of the poet as vestige, as witness: the poet is he or she whose muse has been integrally destroyed.[8] Even so, if one who writes poetry — because despite it all we keep writing poetry — is one whose muse was integrally destroyed, it means that the identity between poet and non poet is never perfect, that it is not possible to integrally destroy the muse, the speaking of the language; something always remains.

To be poet is to be that residue, and from this point of view the line of Hölderlin "but what remains is made by poets"[9] can be

---

[8] Chus Pato. *Hordes of Writing*, transl. by Erín Moure. Exeter: Shearsman Books, 2011, 57.

[9] (IV, 63) "But poets establish what remains." (from "Remembrance," F. Hölderlin, *Hymns and*

read not in the trivial sense that the work of poets will endure in time but that the poetic word is the word that takes on the role of remain or vestige. As such, as a witness to destruction, it names the unforgettable, not in the sense that we have something to remember — though we do — but because it is that residue which gives us shelter, direction, meaning in every way.

To be a residue, witness to a destruction, is to be situated in the place of what was destroyed or never happened (in the skin of a forest, of an ocean, of cut blocks of peat, of the dead, of the ghosts that haunt writing, of utopias) and to bring it newly close to us; it is a type of advance in which a crack, a fissure, sustains what is seen before us.

Fragments, transl. by Richard Sieburth, Princeton: Princeton U Press, 1984. Another possible translation: *But what remains, the poets create.*

A poem is a conjunction of ruins, but these ruins are the drives of the language; they belong to imagination and from there they emit their signals, which desire writing — these ruins are really us navigating birth and emerging into life.

These ruins that are sensitive and in language (symptoms) and that gather and found us are unforgettable, are meaning because they are genesis, are political because they are mind, intelligence (open) // and they are metaphor because they are dislocation, are praxis that unites what is dislocated // sometimes the ruins scare us so we say "I want the ghosts to have hearts" / grass and lichen and always, always birds in symbiosis with horses

it's beauty

and the speed of the otter's wake, though we humans are not overly fond of otters

The poem is an intelligent fissure, it's love that persuades time to exist, time that implants itself into what is to come, primogenital.[10]

---

[10] from Chus Pato, *Secession* (transl. Erín Moure). Toronto: BookThug, 2014, 169.

Aion is a girl who plays dice at the sea's edge[11]

---

[11] *from the Oxford Classical Dictionary, added bu EM*: Aion was personification and god of time indefinitely extended. In early Greek, *αἰών* means 'life' (o 'vital force'), 'whole lifetime,' 'generation.'

There, it wasn't that hard; we only had to conceive of something that exists but is not subject to form, which is to say, that lacks attributes apart from one, which is opposed to all that is raised up or traced; it is illimited and in consequence refractory to the gaze.

It does not oppose what is presented; it surrounds it, traverses it, is anterior and posterior to any object, can't be confused with any object, with persons, with forms, and its possibility, without us deciding that its anteriority is an origin or an original.

They — forms — appear from this illimited, are traced, emerge as figure, exist at the limit that is their trace: a tree, a table, a city, animals, airplanes, nature that conjoins everything we perceive via the senses, hear, see, touch, without this conjunction being its summation; rather it would be its necessity, its liberty of being.

There's nothing beyond that limit, that outline which traces the visible, the world that we think of as technique, as Earthly possibility, as the planet swathed in sky, in a visible veil.

That limit exists and, in contact with it, there's nothing, a nothing that is not limited, not perceptible to the eye, a clarity wrapped around the sky, the planet, that moves between all that is formed, that presents itself out of that which lacks limits, that moves forward, that is perceived and is image, in a concept of image that is bigger than the concept we have when we state that the world is image, a star is image, any body is image.

The image presents, enunciates what is not there, what cannot be retained and is the pulse of any presence.

The image — says Maurice Blanchot — is happy; through it, we believe ourselves masters of absence, but near it abides the nothing. The image is light; the nothing is heavy. From it, the image seems so profound and empty, so threatening and so attractive, rich in meaning and, at once, impoverished and beggarly.

Outside the limit, then, lies that which has no limit, that which cannot be captured in the *éidos*, in form, and it breathes upon what does have form. (I use the word *éidos* in its double sense: as form, such as clock, computer, mountain, any other entity, and as the Platonic Idea in its usual philosophical sense.)

That which cannot be ruled by the Platonic Idea is a happening, a temporality prior to form, and prior to species, even the one we call human or sapiens, prior to our capacity to stand upright, to align our spinal column under our brain, prior to speech, vision, thought, the senses.

Outside the limit, the unformed lies, from there forms emerge, are traced. And this grandeur is not conceived as the negative pole of a speculative dialectic.

The unformed, the halo, the blank page are not synthesized into form, with the formal as apex of a process; rather, blank page and writing continue their becoming, their walk intertwined, coming closer or going farther apart but always retaining their separate characters, like lovers who in embracing refuse to devour or be devoured.

We can conceive of a contact, a touching, a desire of the unformed for form, with each term nonetheless remaining loyal to its own tension.

We think of a flash, spark, a glow that bursts from love, granting the illimited its absence of weight, its transparency, and granting objects — bodies — the quality of weight, gravity, the quality of dissolving into the breath or waft of that which lacks attributes.

I'll propose that the sublime is the fruit of this energy. Just as the previous wing of the butterfly of this discourse spoke of the voice, this second wing will now broach a discussion of the sublime. I'll refer to the writings of Jean-Luc Nancy and Philippe Lacoue-Labarthe.

The notion and choice of the declaration that unites the two wings or chapters of this talk is well known; it comes from an archaic age: "Aion is a girl who plays dice at the sea's edge."

I

Thinking on the sublime is late, born in the heart of Hellenistic schools, very contaminated by Latinity and even by Hebrew and Christian thinking, where the *ho hypsos* designates — for the first diaspora on Greek soil — the God of the Bible, the Most-High.

There's a lesser tradition as well that speaks of the exhaustion of classical beauty, as thinking on excess, on overflowing, on the beyond of the beautiful.

Since Longinus, thinking on the sublime is formulated according to a metaphysical distinction *par excellence*, one that distinguishes between the sensible and the supersensible inherited from Platonism.

Few would object to a definition of the sublime as the presentation of the unpresentable, nuanced by Leotard as the presentation of the fact that there is something unpresentable, or that not everything, the totality, is presentable.

We can think presence in keeping with two apophatic maxims, as figure or as revelation: I'll look at these maxims right away, but before examining the paths where they lead us, I'll summarize the Greek positions regarding the relation between poem and Philosophy. Here, we understand the poem as great poetry, sublime poetry, and as such, the terms poem and sublime will be used interchangeably from here on.

In Parmenides, even mathematical interruptions are recorded under the sacred aura of enunciation. The truth resides in the flesh of the word.

It was Plato who set out the distance between poem and Philosophy.

Aristotle included poetry's knowing in Philosophy, knowledge of all knowledges. This submission of the poem maintains Platonic distance. Including the poem here turns it into an area of thinking that lies under the totalizing umbrella of Philosophy, and this move founds Aesthetics as a discipline.

Heidegger detaches himself from the nuisance of Aesthetics and goes back to Parmenides.

Badiou qualifies the first option as an identificatory rivalry, the second as argumentative distance, and the third as regionalization. The question — which Badiou tries to address in his book *Que pense le poème* — is: how do we get out of Heidegger without going back to Aesthetics?

II

We have at least two formulae, from two traditions, for understanding presence, with two corresponding apophatic maxims:

"Thou shalt not make thee *any* graven image, *or* any likeness *of any thing* that *is* in heaven above, or that *is* in the earth beneath, or that *is* in the waters beneath the earth" (*Deuteronomy 5:8*).

"I am all that has been, that is, and that will be; and no mortal hath ever lifted my veil" (*on the temple of Isis, according to Plutarch*).

In centering ourselves in the first formulation, we are forced to enter the question of limits, of delimitation, of mimesis conceived as reproduction or imitation, which is to say, into that huge discussion in which the pair "material/form" rests on a predetermination of the entity as *éidos*, as figure.

In the interval in which entities or bodies are seen as figures, in the cut or outline of their delimitation, they are divided into limited (material) and limiting (form).

Does this mean that the appearance, revealing, presence,

the *phainesthai* (φαινεσθαι) of the entity, which is to say its luminous and visible being, is derived from that division?

That appearance exists does not depend on eidetic capture of the entity, contrary to Plato. It wasn't Plato who invented the *phainesthai*, the determination of presence via appearance. What Plato did invent, though, is that this appearing occurs in accordance with its Ideal; it's this move, that of the philosopher, that inaugurates Aesthetics.

Hegel (*Aesthetics*), whose thinking seems to differ from the theory of Platonic Ideas, defines the sublime negatively in relation to the beautiful, as the impossibility of representing something that we cannot get close to, an unpresentable *outside*. From this perspective, the sublime offers nothing more than the motif of excess, and nothing less than the motif of the unpresentability of what shows or reveals itself, essentially the concept of beauty, upon which the sublime is still dependent.

Hegel thought of the sublime as a dialectical presentation, negative and restrictive.

If the sublime is the inadequation of form to content, and beauty is the figural reconciliation of spirit and form, we might think of the sublime as an interval prior to beauty. It's a counter-concept of the beautiful: as such, we can affirm that the sublime is the first level of beauty. (In the famous line of Rilke, these premises act in inversion: "For beauty is nothing but the beginning of terror we are scarcely able to endure," and here we can also add that, in the tradition of Burke, the terrible is a word for the sublime.)

It doesn't escape us that conciliation of the sensible and the supersensible — and the spiritual conformity of form — require here, just as in Plato, an eidetic capture of the entity.

Of course, if the infinite is presented as delimited and finite form, the sublime is shown to us in its contradictory structure; from this we have the maxim of Hegel's *Aesthetics*: "the manifestation of the infinite annihilates the manifestation itself."[12]

At this point in the question, we can consider the following: either Hegel is right and negative presentation signifies the negation of presentation, the poetics of silence (thus no poem may be written, no *sublime* poem, after Auschwitz, and any attempt to do so is doomed to be exhausted in the presentation of its own impossibility), or: the poem, the sublime art, is not essentially a matter of

---

[12] Philippe Lacoue-Labarthe. "Sublime Truth" in *Of the Sublime: Presence in Question*. 71-108. Transl. Jeffrey S. Librett. Albany: SUNY Press, 1993, 95.

eidetic presentation, whether dialectic or Platonic.

It's time to ask, as well, what kind of writing would be the ideal to which all other compositions, given their capture by the *éidos*, might aspire, even if they'll never be more than pale copies or imitations of the Idea-poem. I won't answer the question; I'll just note that some texts that present themselves to us as secular have never managed to free themselves from their religious matrix, neither in the conception of the poem nor in the model of the poet, whether this be christly (messianic) or apostolic, or by imitation or rejection.

Finally, I ask: what would a *non eidetic* presentation be, Platonically speaking, of the entity recognizable as poem, of the sublime art, of any type of entity, of a tree, an animal, a city, an airplane?

In *The Meridian*, previously quoted, Paul Celan writes: *"The absolute poem — no, it certainly does not, cannot exist. But in every real poem, even the least ambitious, there is this ineluctable question, this exorbitant claim."*[13]

III

I'll abandon the first apophatic maxim now to focus on the second, the inscription on the temple of Isis: "I am all that has been, that is, and that will be; and no mortal hath ever lifted my veil."

In contrast with Mosaic enunciation, that of the temple of Isis is not prescriptive, but declarative: it sustains that it is not possible to pull the veil from the essence of divinity.

It speaks, as does the Biblical enunciation, of metaphysical un-

---

[13] Paul Celan "The Meridian," in *Collected Prose*. Transl. Rosemarie Waldrop. NY: Routledge, 2006: 51.

presentability, understood as truth or essence of the *physis*. It affirms that something like the unpresentable exists. And this unpresentable is thought of as veiled.

Its form is well known: *I, the truth, speak. I, the truth, speak the truth and say that the truth remains veiled*, from which we can see that the sentence is roundly sublime. It involves a contradictory enunciation, the syntactical equivalent of an oxymoron.

The oxymoron seems to confirm the Hegelian thesis on Egypt, with Egypt seen as a step to the zenith, which is Greece. In Egypt, the spirit makes stone sing, but remains trapped in the shadow of the Colossi of Memnon. To Hegel, the Greeks, who freed the spirit, were naturally the sun at its zenith. Truth is the pure removal of the veil, the exit from night, from the feminine, from the land of the dead, from Egypt, from the pure glare of the sun.

On the contrary, for Kant, no sun dissipates the veil of the divinity. The sentence generates only a holy shiver. Truth, in its essence — and here we move on from what we've said about mystery and the ethics of mystery — is non-truth; truth cannot be spoken in its totality, what happens is that at some point, it abandons its own blind spot, which we call the unsayable.

That truth has its base or *razón* in non-truth leads us to a contradictory structure, that of *a-letheia*: its *razón* is *lethe*. An entity is never without veil, and neither is a poem.

The halo, the blank page, the canvas would be the very condition of what has no veil, of an emptiness that is never a given thing, a pure temporality.

This temporality is never an apparition, and is not presentation;

we know this because the entity (language), in its very familiarity, suddenly finds itself estranged.

The blank page is that estrangement.

The native, nature, the entity, language, the tree, the native is estranged, is the strange.

The blank page is the experience of the sublime in and of itself.

Impulse that produces the poem, estrangement of the entity, of language, this is *ek-tase* or rapture. This precipitation outside the self, as Burke put it, and which has been described from Longinus to Boileau and from Fénelon to Kant, is the emotion or affect of the truly sublime.

It takes place in this experience of presentation, when what strikes us is that there is an entity and not nothing. There is articulated language in our species and not nothing; there is the poem and not nothing.

In other words, presentation as figuration — as *éidos*, as Aesthetics — becomes secondary.

Before one entity or another (articulated language or not, a petal, a building) stands out for us, or before we can even begin to imagine something like an entity standing out on a background without depth, there is the simple fact of the entity, and this is what a poem offers, its appearance, its arrival in the world, its nativity.

It doesn't just stand out, it scintillates, it radiates in the night without night, in the beyond of the night of nothingness, this which is halo, emptiness, nothing that is, a depth without depth; as we've said, it is refractory to presence: it glows, resplendent, is a beyond of the night of nothingness.

And it is deep affirmation, such that in the apprehension of the sublime no dialectic, no Aesthetics take place.

The sublime, from this perspective, would be the presentation of the fact that there is presentation. It is an affirmative comprehension of the sublime, of the poem.

Perhaps the meditation on the sublime stems from the desire to find what in beauty is irreducible to its capture in the Platonic Idea, the "je ne sais quoi" of which Juan de la Cruz writes, or that of which Xosé Luís Méndez Ferrín, in these lines, wisely warns us:

This is the river in which any who attempt
to form raptures, sustenance, signs,
will get nothing back but a kick in the gut
and the ancient woe of feeling dismissed

Velaquí o río no que quenqueira que intente
formar raptos, sostemento, signos,
non collerá outra cousa ca un couce no bandullo
e a tristura antiquísima de se sentir disolto

that beam, extreme light, brightness of appearance itself.

IV

It is time to consider more broadly the *razón* of the poem, and ask under what conditions the sublime poem is possible.

The innate is that which is *physis*; it is the gift of nature. It is all that in art (*téchne*) touches *physis* itself, and here we arrive at the question of genius and how in Kant and Nietzsche the theme of the sublime will unfold.

Genius is what rules art.

Ingenuity, genius, the ingenious, is the innate disposition of the spirit through which nature rules art.

Longinus wrote of exactly this: of immense nature, its incredible gifts, gifts from the heavens.

How to affirm that the sublime touches, at the same time, on *physis* (on genius) and on *téchne*?

In matters of the sublime, nature is autonomous; it has its own law. Natural gifts are regulated; genius follows the rules of nature.

Measure, the sense of the opportune moment, a sureness in practice — all this is calculated and learned, as Hölderlin tells us.

All gifts of nature or of the gods, all favourable fate, are nothing if the right decision is not made. This structure, writes Longinus, regulates the relation between nature and technique, art, *poiesis*, poem.

In Aristotle, *téchne* is literally seen as an addition to nature, which is to say, appearance is like growing, budding, or coming to light. Technique, art, the muses, only these are able to reveal nature. Without them, without the muses, *physis* is veiled — and it does love going into hiding, going mute.

It is this that we understand when Aristotle, in discussing poetry in Chapter IV of the *Poetics*, defines *téchne* or technique, which is to say mimesis, as representation, as presence, as grasping the present.

Technique is the production (*poiesis*) of knowledge. This knowledge appears via mimesis in that mimesis is the faculty of grasping the present in general and not the faculty of reproduction, of reduplication and even less of copying or imitating in general.

Mimesis is the faculty of grasping the presence of that which, without it, would remain encrypted.

This knowledge in Longinus is opposed to and resists the Platonic view of mimesis.

Technique, art, mimesis are gifts of nature to being to allow it to appear, to make present its very being.

So, now, how to awaken this gift in us?

The Kantian answer would surely point to mimetic contagion. The genius (ingenious) is that person whom great poetry, great art, impresses.

Physis gives birth in our soul, writes Longinus, to an invincible eros for all that is greater and more divine that we ourselves are.

Longinus conceives of us as meta-ontic beings; he conceives *physis* as being, and sustains that our thoughts surpass the limits that contain us. To him, it is in this that we recognize the *razón* for which we are born. Which is, in fact: appearance, this surpassing.

V

The natal,[14] "native" or "proper to onself" is all that which, though

---

[14] from Hölderlin's *Nationelle*, what is proper to a thing in and of itself, a birthright, "by birth."

its destiny is to stay hidden or secret, comes to light. In Hölderlin we learn of the risk that ensues from this arrival into the world of what is meant to persist in secret: "Nothing is more difficult than the free use of the natal.[15]"

---

[15] Pato: "Nada é máis difícil que o libre uso do natal". *Wir lernen nichts schwerer als das Nationelle frei gebrauchen. The hardest thing to learn is the free use of the national.* Hölderlin used "Nationelle" at a time when a modern view of nation was emerging (so it would be anachronistic to see the word just through our eyes, with no further advisement). As such, it has been translated variously into English as "the national," "national traits," "the proper." A neologism, it is used by Hölderlin to indicate what is socially, culturally, politically proper to poetry. A birthright, in itself, perhaps. In the words of William Allen, "as a later paraphrase of this line indicates, 'the free use of what is one's own,' we should not look to the modern political meaning of 'national,' but to the chiasmic translation of our own nature." To Allen, "the 'Nationelle'... is a radical impropriety... which might explain why it is that which, in being what is most one's own, is also what is most difficult to learn."

Supra luz, this appearance is the strange clarity of being itself, the night that blinds us, the dark lightning in the poetry of Pondal, the sober clarity of which Hölderlin spoke, beyond all and any light.

The sublime would be the presentation of freedom, insofar as it is concerned with the illimited.

The sublime is that which arises at the edge of the limit, of the schema, of figure, form, presence, phenomenon, of appearance.

It has no beginning, never ends, is not dialectic: it is a cut, a caesura, a fissure.

It is not a number; it is a gesture from the infinite, the gesture through which all finite form arises in the absence of form, prior to figuration, a presentation without presentation, an overflow of the limit, the border, its release.

Its logic is that of being at the limit of the imagination, of mimesis.

VI

That articulated language exists is sublime; the sublime is that a poem arises, the illimited of the beauty of a language, the incomparability of that language, that the grandeur of a language exists, that there exists a limit that arises, a multiplicity presenting itself as figure, as poem.

VII

Totality is not the totality of the infinite; it is that of the illimited, of what's on the far side of the limit, beyond the maximal, beyond the everything.

Imagination, mimesis, sense this limit which is maximal and minimal in that they imagine and touch the limit.

In the sublime, the limit does not cede, does not remit; it presents itself as a syncope, a suspension of imagination/of language, as that interruption in which the limit traces itself and becomes figure.

The blankness suspends in the heavens, on the blank screen.

The sublime is caesura, a vanishing/dissolving of the language in the illimited, the emotion of a speech/writing right at the limit.

Thus articulated language, the conjunction of all possible spoken or written propositions (its totality is not configured by adding up all these propositions, but rather by their onticity) which is, as with all technique or art or mimesis, placed by nature in the human species, illimited and infinite, loves or is loved by breath, also known as halo or aura or void or neuter or the pure temporality — *Aion* — that is Being refractory to presence and without attributes.

There the writing of a language realizes its limit, it knows it, it experiences it via imagination, which is the faculty of mimesis or art.

At the limit, held at that very limit, a poem blossoms or can blossom, a poem that is figure arisen, traced, and also infinite, excellence, entelechy, and — in contact with breath or *aion* — remains exposed to that which has no limit, form, word, colour, or sound.

To experience this love.

This beauty of the poem would be that of a thing, a living thing that, produced by mimesis and therefore an *éidos*, a figure, would be open to what lacks presence, would be a self-determined artefact which, being infinite and limited, exposes itself to what lacks limits: an infinite opening to an illimited.

It returns again and again, in its difference it composes, executes its own model every time, returning, incessant, poeticizing its *razzo*, its *ditamen*.

An oxymoron, a perfect paradox.

The infinite exposed/open to the girl who plays dice at the sea's edge, at the oceanLimit

*   *   *

Your Excellencies, I am honoured today to assume the academic chair once held by Xosé Fernández Ferreiro, which links me to the Miño River — land of my father — and by Francisco Del Riego, who opened the doors of this Academy to Galicians and to the world; it was held, too, by Florentino Cuevillas,[16]

---

[16] *Xosé Fernández Ferreiro* (1931-2015). Writer and journalist, member of the Brais Pinto group. *Francisco Fernández Del Riego* (1913-2010). Thinker, writer, founder of the publisher Galaxia. *Florentino López Cuevillas* (1886-1958). Writer, historian,

so present in this city of Ourense and in the memory of Ourensans, and by Uxío Carré Aldao, exemplary publisher of works in Galician and a founder of this Academy.

I confess that since I found out that my investiture would take place in the Auditorium of the Instituto Otero Pedrayo in Ourense, I heard inside me the voices of three beloved friends who very sadly are unable to join us: the unforgettable Belén Feliú, my adored Begoña de Saa, and Sabela R. Oxea,[17] epitome of perfection and beauty. All three women taught here. Along with their voices, I hear that of a man who once taught me here. I can't claim to have been a good student;

---

archaeologist, member of Generation Nós. *Uxío Carré Aldao* (1859-1932). Writer, bookseller, publisher.

[17] *Belén Moreno Feliú* (1961-1997), critic, writer, teacher. *Begoña Muñoz Saa* (1961-2010), dramatist, teacher. *Sabela Rodríguez Oxea* (1958-2012), poet and teacher.

even so, the lessons that I learned burn in my heart and memory for eternity. Today I name, with gratitude, Xesús Ferro Couselo,[18] the academician who, on a cold morning now distant in time, swore to the police that I had been in his classroom. That day, although I was not among those who were passing out pamphlets of the Unión do Pobo Galego (UPG — Union of the Galician People),[19] I was acting as a lookout so that they could be distributed. Clearly, I was not doing this from inside his classroom. Ferro Couselo's act, as well as being

---

[18] *Xesús Ferro Couselo* (1909-1975). Historian, archaeologist, political thinker, museologist, writer, teacher, priest who made great cultural and scholarly contributions to Galician letters.

[19] A Galician nationalist and communist political party started in 1963 during the Francoist dictatorship, calling for self-determination of the Galician people and a federation with the other peoples of Spain. It is still active today as a party that acts within the framework of the Spanish Constitution.

one of solidarity, exemplifies what it really means to teach Philosophy.

My profound thanks as well go to Xosé Luís Méndez Ferrín who, here in Ourense, our native city, during a protest one afternoon in 1986 against the entry of the Spanish State into NATO, confirmed my vocation as an aspiring poet.

To Xabier Cordal, for his friendship.

To Erín Moure, for working to promote Galician literature in her community and wherever she goes.

To my publisher, Carlos Lema, for his jovial impatience.

To the Amiable Gentleman, Arturo Casas, for his unerring judgement and kindness.

To Iris Cochón, always.

Ladies and gentlemen, dearest friends, I am now at the end of my inaugural speech upon becoming a member of the Royal Galician

Academy. It is an event that will forever cleave my body in two, that of an academician and that of the person I am.

To close, I would like to read a poem from *Memorial and Dance*[20] by Francisco Cortegoso, a poet who left us recently, and far too soon.

DEDICATION

Out there where language lets go,
and thus all material is in expansion,
there where language becomes transparent,
passes through itself, dies down,
and takes on sound, and silence;
there it touches itself, as in a palimpsest,
and goes out and lights up like nothing,
breaks, turns back on itself
in its ordering;
here, fallen, in returning to the world,
it occludes, is traversed. Greater than light or shadow.
And always for each one of us, humans, the loss
    / or expansion of movement, in us.
This very breath.
So we will not be lost.

---

[20] Francisco Cortegoso, 1985-2016. *Memorial e danza.* Culleredo, Galicia: Espiral Maior, 2014.

To end in my language, Galician, I offer Francisco Cortegoso's poem in the original:

DEDICACIÓN

Alí onde a lingua perde lugar,
e así a materia toda se expande,
onde se transparenta,
se traspasa a si propia, se mata,
e toma son, e o silencio;
aí que acada si propia, como nun palimpsesto,
e se apaga e esclarece como nada,
rota, volta sobre si
ordenándose;
aquí, caída, por se devolver ao mundo;
oclúe, atravésase. Maior que a luz nin sombra.
E sempre para cada un de nós, humanos, a perda
       /ou inflación do movemento, en nós.
A esta respiración.
Por non perdermos.

September 23, 2017
Ourense
Galicia

Chus Pato teaches history and geography in Lalín, a small city in Galicia (NW Spain), and writes in the Galician language. Her sixth book of poetry and first in her pentalogy *Decrúa (Delve)*, *m-Talá*, broke the poetic mould in Galicia in 2000. All five books of the pentalogy have been translated by Erín Moure into English: *m-Talá*, *Charenton*, *Hordes of Writing*, *Secession* (published with *Insecession* by Erín Moure), and *Flesh of Leviathan*. The original *Hordes of Writing* in Galician received the Spanish Critics' Prize in 2008 and the Losada Diéguez Prize in 2009. In 2013, the Galician Booksellers' Association fêted Chus Pato as Author of the Year. In 2015, she became the first Galician voice in the sound archives of the Woodberry Poetry Library at Harvard University. Her *Collected Poems* came out in two volumes in Spanish translation in Barcelona in 2017, the year she entered the Royal Galician Academy. Her latest book, *Un Libre Favor*, appeared in spring 2019 to great acclaim. She performs and speaks regularly at literary festivals and conferences in Europe and in South America, and has also appeared in Canada, USA, Cuba, and North Africa. In November 2019, she will be an invited guest at Queen's College, University of Oxford.

Erín Moure is a poet and translator of poetry and poetics. In Canada, USA, and UK (variously), she has published 19 books of poetry, a volume of essays, a book of articles on translation, and two memoirs, and she is translator or co-translator of 17 books of poetry and 5 of non-fiction (biopoetics and memoir) from French, Spanish, Galician, and Portuguese. In Canada, her work has received the Governor General's Award, Pat Lowther Memorial Award, A.M. Klein Prize twice, and has been a three-time finalist for the Griffin Prize (two of these for translation). Among recent works are *Insecession* (BookThug, 2014), a biopoetics in one volume with, and in response to, Chus Pato's *Secession*, and *Kapusta* (Anansi, 2015). New in 2016 are translations of François Turcot's *My Dinosaur* (BookThug), Chus Pato's *Flesh of Leviathan* (Omnidawn), and Rosalía de Castro's *New Leaves* (Small Stations). A 40-year retrospective, *Planetary Noise: The Poetry of Erín Moure* (edited and introduced by Shannon Maguire), came out from Wesleyan University Press in 2017, the year which also saw the appearance of her translation from portunhol of Wilson Bueno's *Paraguayan Sea* (Nightboat Books, finalist Best Translated Book Award), and a translation from Galician of Antón Lopo's *Distance of the Wolf: A biography of Uxío Novoneyra* (Fundación Uxío Novoneyra). 2019 saw a translation from Galician of Lupe Gómez's *Camouflage* (Circumference Books), a co-translation with Roman Ivashkiv of Yuri Izdryk's *Smokes* (Lost Horse Press) and her own *The Elements* (Anansi). Moure continues to write and translate in Montreal.

www.ingramcontent.com/pod-product-compliance
Lightning Source LLC
Chambersburg PA
CBHW071408040426
42444CB00009B/2151